Mary Alice Fontenot

Clovis Crawfish and the Singing Cigales

Illustrated by Eric Vincent

PELICAN PUBLISHING COMPANY
GRETNA 1999

First edition, 1965
Second edition, 1981
Third printing, 1999

For Robert Gilmore and Myrta Fair Craig
Parrain and *Marraine* of the Cicada Twins
Chicot and Coteau Cigale de Bois

Library of Congress Cataloging in Publication Data

Fontenot, Mary Alice.
    Clovis Crawfish and the singing Cigales.

    Summary: Clovis Crawfish and his friends meet two
singing cicadas and outfox the bully M'sieu Blue Jay.
    [1. Bayous--Fiction.   2. Animals--Fiction]
I. Vincent, Eric.   II. Title.
PZ7.F73575Cm   [Fic]   81-5608
ISBN   0-88289-270-3   AACR2

Printed in Singapore

Published by Pelican Publishing Company, Inc.
1000 Burmaster Street, Gretna, Louisiana 70053

Design and production by Eric Vincent

It was summertime on the bayou where Clovis Crawfish lived.
Clovis was 'way down deep in the hole underneath his mud
house. His big, sharp claws were closed. His long whiskers were
not wiggling. Clovis Crawfish was sound asleep.

M'sieu Blue Jay flew over the bayou with an acorn in his beak. Just as he passed over Clovis Crawfish's mud house he dropped the acorn, and it fell right into the round hole in the top of Clovis' house.

The acorn rolled down, down, down into the hole. It hit Clovis *ker-flunk!* right on the head. Clovis woke up.

"Who did that?" he exclaimed.

Clovis Crawfish backed up. He raised up his big, sharp claws and twitched his whiskers.

"*Jamais de la vie!*" cried Clovis, which is the way to say "Never in my life!" in French. He crawled straight up through the round hole in his mud house and out onto the bayou bank.

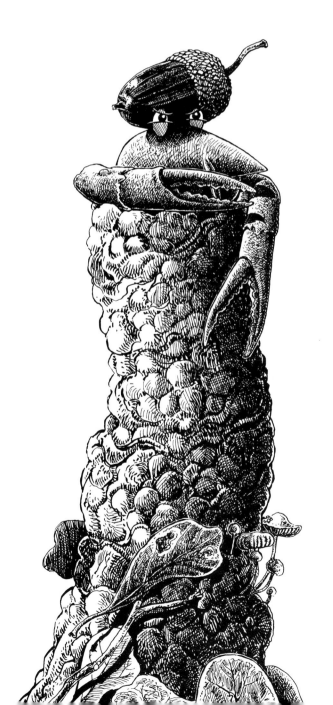

René Rain Frog was up in the muscadine vine singing his rain song: "*J'ai chaud! J'ai chaud! J'ai chaud!*" which means "I'm hot! I'm hot! I'm hot!"

Christophe Cricket peeped out from under the root of the live oak tree. *"Moi aussi! Moi aussi! Moi aussi!"* chirped Christophe, which is the way to say "Me too! Me too! Me too!" in French.

A fat green cicada with see-through wings was clinging to the bark of the live oak tree. The cicada rustled its wings and looked at Clovis Crawfish.

Clovis flexed his claws. "Did you drop that acorn on me?" he asked the cicada.

"Who, me?" said the cicada. "*Mais non!* I just got here. My name is Chicot Cigale de Bois, and I'm waiting for my brother, Coteau Cigale de Bois, so we can have our summer concert. We are singers. We just love to sing!"

A brown creature-thing with no wings was on the tree bark beside Chicot Cigale.

"Who's that?" asked Clovis, pointing his claw at the brown thing.

"That's not a 'who.' That's a 'what,'" said Chicot Cigale. That's my old shell! It used to be a 'who'—it was me when I lived in the ground!"

"*Mais jamais!*" exclaimed Clovis, which means "You don't say!" in Acadian-French. "But you're twice as big as your old shell. Wasn't it crowded in there for you?"

"Yes, it was," said Chicot Cigale. "Especially when I started growing. I got too big for my skin! So I crawled out of the ground and squeezed out. See that crack in the top of my old shell? That's where I got out!"

"*C'est drôle!*" said Clovis, which means "How strange!" in French. "Does your brother look like you?"

"But of course!" said Chicot Cigale. "We're twins! He looks just like me. That is, he will when he gets out of his old shell. And he will have long, beautiful wings just like mine. Then we can sing and sing and sing!"

Bertile Butterfly flitted by on her way to the honeysuckle vine. Maurice Mosquito Hawk sat perfectly still on top of the thistle. Denis Dirt Dauber buzzed down to the edge of the bayou for a load of wet mud.

"Look!" cried Chicot Cigale. "There's my brother! There's Coteau Cigale crawling out of that hole by the tree trunk!"

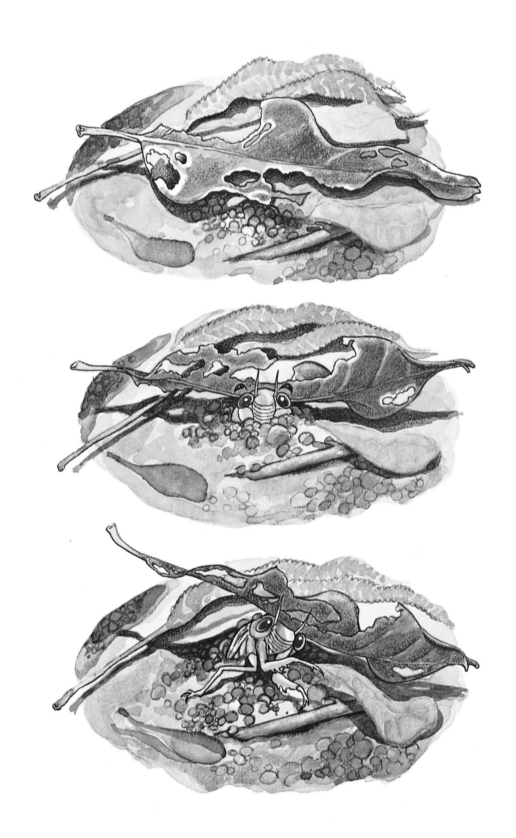

Clovis and his friends watched while a brown bug squirmed out of the hole and crawled up the tree trunk. The bug looked exactly like Chicot Cigale's old shell. Soon the top of the shell split open and Coteau Cigale began to squeeze himself out.

Lizette Lizard ran down the tree trunk. *"Pauvre 'tite bête!"* said Lizette, which means "Poor little thing!" in Acadian-French. "How will he ever get through that tiny crack? Can't you help him, Clovis?"

"Don't worry Lizette. He'll get out," said Clovis. "Chicot Cigale got out, so Coteau Cigale will also. You'll see!"

"Then we can have our concert!" said Chicot Cigale. "Only we'll have to wait 'til Coteau Cigale's wings get dry. He can't fly around 'til his wings are dry. That's when we will sing and sing and sing!"

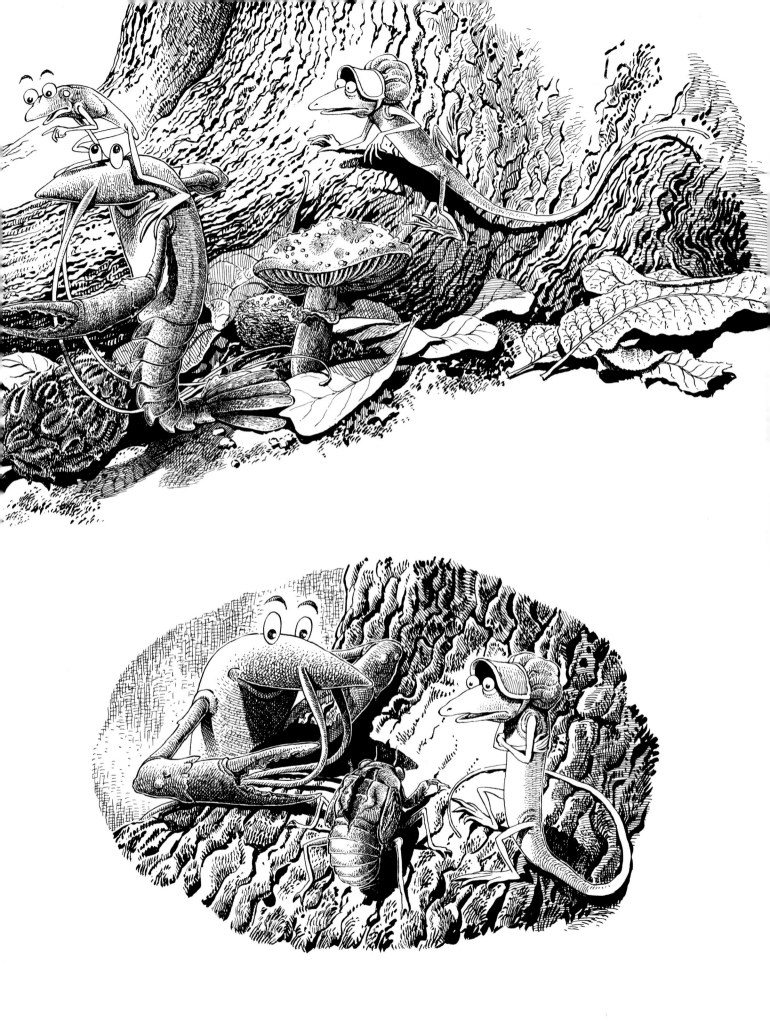

"I can sing," said Fernand Frog in his big, deep voice.

"*Moi aussi,*" said Christophe Cricket.

"I sing for rain," said René Rain Frog.

Bertile Butterfly fluttered her pretty wings. "*J'aime les fleurs,*" said Bertile, which means "I like flowers."

"I can change my color," said Lizette Lizard. She ran down onto the grass and her color changed from brown to green.

"I build houses with wet mud," said Denis
Dirt Dauber.

"I have a thousand eyes," said Maurice
Mosquito Hawk.

Chicot Cigale flew around in great excitement.
"Look! Look!" cried Chicot. "Coteau is almost out!"

Just then M'sieu Blue Jay flew back from across the bayou and perched in the magnolia tree.

"Chee-ANK! Chee-ANK!" he squawked.

"Hide yourselves!" cried Clovis. "Quick! Hide before M'sieu
Jay eats you!"

Christophe Cricket backed up into his hole under the root of
the live oak tree.

Lizette Lizard ran up the tree trunk and turned brown.

René Rain Frog slithered around on the under side of the pal-
metto plant.

Chicot Cigale sat on the limb and trembled.

"Come on, Chicot! Hide!" cried Clovis.

"But what about my brother?" said Chicot. "Coteau can't
hide! He's only half out of the shell! He can't fly 'til his wings
get dry!"

"Chee-ANK! Chee-ANK!" squawked M'sieu Blue Jay. He spotted poor helpless Coteau Cigale clinging to the tree trunk, halfway out of his old shell. One of his wings was sticking out of the shell, crumpled up and sticky.

M'sieu Jay swooped down, grabbed the old shell with Coteau in it, and took off across the bayou.

Chicot Cigale cried and cried. "My poor brother! I can't sing! I can't sing! I can't sing ever again!"

Just then Clovis Crawfish and his friends heard a loud shrill humming. The humming sound got louder and louder.

Chicot Cigale stopped crying and listened. "That's Coteau!" he cried. "I know it's Coteau!"

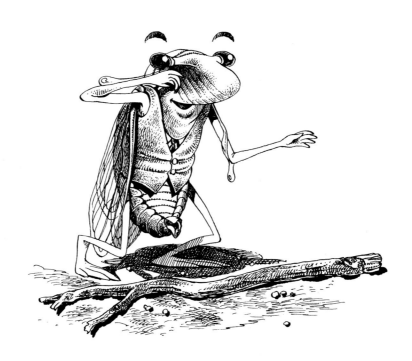

Coteau Cigale flew in and lit on top of Clovis' mud house.

"I got away!" he said. "That old bird dropped me in the middle of his nest, and the greedy baby birds started to fight about which one was going to eat me! While they were fighting I squeezed out of my shell, my wings dried out, and I flew away!"

"Now we can have the concert?" said Fernand Frog in his big, deep voice.

"*Pas encore!*" said Clovis Crawfish, which means "Not yet!" in French. "M'sieu Blue Jay will come back when he finds out Coteau got away!"

"But what can we do?" asked Chicot Cigale. "We have to sing!"

"But yes!" cried Coteau Cigale. "We just have to sing!"

Clovis wiggled his whiskers. "Maybe we can play a trick on that *canaille* old bird!" he said. "Denis, bring me some mud! Lizette, find two green leaves!"

Denis Dirt Dauber made a hundred and sixteen trips back and forth from the bayou to the tree trunk, hauling wet mud. He carefully stuffed the mud into Chicot Cigale's empty shell. Lizette Lizard brought two slender leaves, and Clovis stuck them into the slit in Coteau's old shell.

"*Voilà!*" exclaimed Clovis. "That should fool even M'sieu Jay!"

Maurice Mosquito Hawk lit on the thistle. Chicot and Coteau sat on a branch of the big oak, waiting to start the concert. Fernand Frog was on the bayou bank practicing his bass notes. Christophe Cricket tuned up for his chirping solo.

"Chee-ANK! Chee-ANK!" squawked M'sieu Blue Jay as he came flying in.

Chicot and Coteau Cigale flew up and hid themselves in the Spanish moss hanging from the oak tree. Lizette Lizard, René Rain Frog, and Christophe Cricket took off in different directions.

M'sieu Blue Jay flew down and hopped around on the ground, looking for Coteau Cigale. He spied Chicot Cigale's old shell clinging to the tree trunk. It looked just like a live *cigale de bois*. He pounced on it, the empty shell crunched, and he got a beakful of sticky mud.

"Chee-ANK! Chee-ANK!"

M'sieu Blue Jay was so furious he flew off in a huff, 'way across the bayou.

"Now we can have the concert!" announced Clovis Crawfish.
"*Allons chanter!*" which means "Let's sing!" in French.

Les Beaux Jours de l'Été*

Piano Arrangement by
Anne-Marie Landry

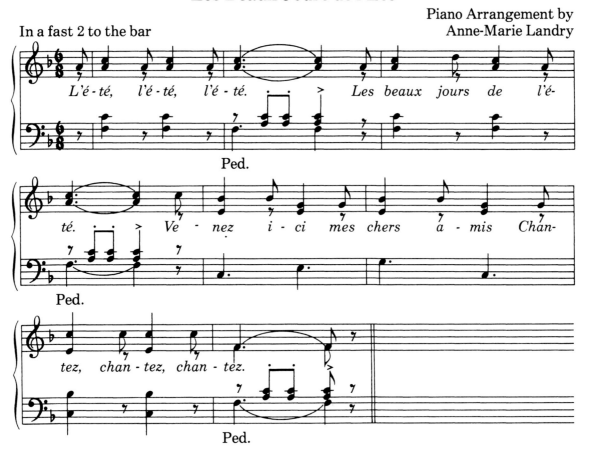

*Literal translation: Summer, summer, summer. The beautiful days of summer.
Come here my dear friends. Sing, Sing, Sing!